Cor

CW01095301

What is a game changer?

Game changers are people who use their skills, talents and ideas to change the world. Some of their ideas are so original that it takes time for the world to catch up. But when it does, the world is changed forever.

The computer wizards

Technology has made our lives so easy. We can play games and send information around the world in seconds! In this book, we admire the people who helped make that happen. Some invented the technology, some made it easier to use – either way, they were game changers.

Grace Hopper

(1906–1992)

"I've always been more interested in the future than the past."

Grace Hopper

Grace Hopper was a true game changer. She was a computer scientist who **revolutionised** the way we think about computers and what they can do. She did all of this while working for the US Navy and spending time encouraging young people – especially girls – to follow in her footsteps. She was a **formidable** woman with a powerful personality – they even named a battleship after her.

USS Hopper

Grace was born in New York, USA. She was interested in mathematics from an early age, and when she graduated from college, she became a maths teacher. When the USA joined the Second World War in 1941, she tried to join the Navy. However, they said she was too old and too short. She tried again, and in 1944 she was **enlisted** to program computers for the war.

Did you know?

People say that when she was young, Grace took apart seven alarm clocks to see how they worked!

The Navy sent Grace to Harvard University to help program the Mark I Computer. In the 1940s, computers were much bigger than they are now – and much less powerful.

The Mark I

A room-sized mechanical computer.

Built by the famous computer company, IBM®.

Weighed four tonnes – about as heavy as a hippo!

Used by the USA to make calculations during the Second World War.

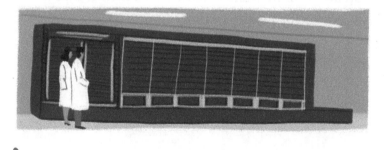

Grace spent the war helping with calculations, including ones that were used to make the first **atomic bomb**.

After the war, Grace began to think of new ways to use computers. She thought that more people would use computers if they were less complicated to program.

Grace began working on a new computer language that everyone could use. It used English words instead of mathematical sums. This meant that it was easier for people to understand.

This language was used to develop COBOL (the Common Business Orientated Language) which is still used to this day. Without it, computers may have remained too complicated, and would never have found their way into every corner of our lives.

Grace continued her work with computer languages until her death in 1992.

Did you know?

When Grace retired from the Navy in 1986 aged 80, she was the oldest serving officer in the US Military.

Grace was a game changer. She took something that existed and made it simpler to use. On top of that, she worked to make sure that the next generation of computer programmers was ready to follow in her footsteps. She spoke at schools around the USA and inspired many people.

Every year, an award is given in her name to a young computer professional who has made a difference in the world of computing.

Did you know?

Her nickname was 'Amazing Grace' — she earned it!

Shigeru Miyamoto

(1952–)

"I'd like to be known as the person who saw things from a different point of view."

Shigeru Miyamoto

You've probably played a computer game that Shigeru Miyamoto helped to create. Shigeru is known as the father of modern computer games. Through his work with Nintendo™, he has invented some of the best-loved characters and games in the world.

Shigeru's best-known games:

- → Super Mario Brothers™
- → The Legend of Zelda™
- → Star Fox™
- → Donkey Kong™
- → Nintendogs™

Shigeru was born in Japan. He grew up in a house without a television, and so was always making his own fun. As a boy, he would make his own toys out of wood and string, and put on puppet shows for his family. He was used to making things to play with – perfect for a game designer. However, he didn't set out to be a game designer. He wanted to be an illustrator when he grew up.

When Shigeru joined Nintendo in 1977, the company made playing cards and arcade games.
Shigeru still wanted to be an artist, so he started his career designing the cabinets for Nintendo's arcade games.

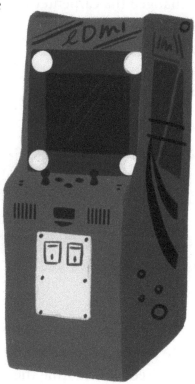

In 1981, Shigeru made the move from designing cabinets to designing the actual arcade games. He didn't have the technical knowledge, but he knew how to write a story and create characters that gamers would care about.

Did you know?

Shigeru's first game was Donkey Kong™.

Donkey Kong™ featured a carpenter rescuing a princess from a gorilla. For his next game, Shigeru changed the carpenter into a plumber, and Super Mario™ was born!

Shigeru often takes inspiration from his personal life for his games. The Legend of Zelda™ was inspired by exploring the countryside as a boy. Nintendogs™ was inspired by the time he and his family bought a dog.

Did you know?

To date, over 400 million games featuring the character Mario have been sold.

Shigeru had a hand in helping to create Pokémon™ when he **mentored** Pokémon creator, Satoshi Tajiri. There is even a Pokémon character named after him!

Shigeru is still inventing games to this day. He tries out all of the games he invents first. He believes that if he enjoys it, then others will too. Who knows what game-changing character he has up his sleeve next! Chances are they will be coming to a gaming screen near you very soon.

What makes Shigeru a game changer is the way he brought characters and a story to video games. Believe it or not, it was rare for video games to have them before Shigeru.

The key to a successful Shigeru game:

character — someone gamers care about

story — gamers want to know what is going to happen next

adventure — gamers love to be taken to new places.

Shigeru has changed computer games. He is quite literally a game changer!

Susan Kare

(1954–)

"Icon design is ... trying to marry an image and idea that ideally will be easy for people to understand and remember."

Susan Kare

The story of technology is often the story of people finding small ways to make a big difference. Grace Hopper invented an easier computer programming language. Grace's language allowed us to ask computers to do things. Susan Kare went one step further. She designed pictures that meant we didn't have to ask at all – we just clicked!

Susan was born in New York, USA in 1954. She started working for Apple® in 1982. At that time, Apple was a technology company working on making a home computer.

It was her job to design the **icons** – or little pictures – that users clicked on to launch a program. If you wanted to draw, you clicked on a paintbrush; if you wanted to cut, you clicked on scissors; and if you wanted to put something in the bin, you clicked on the recycling bin.

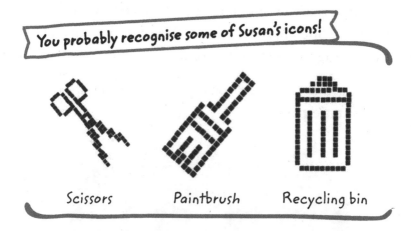

You probably recognise some of Susan's icons!

Scissors   Paintbrush   Recycling bin

Before Susan created her icons, if you wanted a computer to do something, you had to learn the programming language and type commands into a screen. It is much easier to see a picture of what you want and click on it to make it happen. Susan's icons made computers much easier to use.

Susan was an artist before she was a computer scientist. She approached the idea of designing icons by looking to artists of the past.

At that time, computer pictures were made up of tiny square **pixels**.

Susan thought that using squares to create a picture was a lot like making a mosaic out of tiles. Susan bought some graph paper and, by colouring in the little squares, she created blocky images that could be transferred on to the screen.

Susan had to keep the images simple enough so that they could be seen and understood on the screen. She also had to design images that everyone would recognise no matter where in the world they came from.

Her designs were used by Apple for years, and versions of them are still used to this day.

After working for Apple, Susan moved to Microsoft™ and designed similar icons for the Windows™ operating system used on computers all over the world.

Susan is a game changer. Thanks to her, you no longer needed to be an expert in order to use a computer. Her easy-to-use icons influenced the way modern laptops, tablets and phones work. Next time you click, think of Susan – if she didn't design the icon herself she probably inspired it!

Did you know?

In 2015, the New York Museum of Modern Art put Susan's sketches of the original Apple Macintosh® icons on display in their gallery.

Steve Jobs

(1955–2011)

"Our goal is to make the best devices in the world."

Steve Jobs

When Susan Kare worked at Apple, it was a company making computers for the home. In the 35 years since then, it has become famous for making many more things. From computers, to tablets, to phones, people all over the world rely on Apple devices. The man who brought them to the wider world was Steve Jobs. He didn't invent everything Apple made, but he knew how to make people want them.

Steve was born in San Francisco, USA. Life wasn't always easy for him. He was adopted shortly after he was born and struggled with school. He didn't do well in lessons and often played tricks rather than pay attention to what the teachers had to say. Some say that this was because he liked making people laugh, but others say that he was so clever he was often bored.

Steve Jobs as a boy

Top Tip

Don't try using that excuse yourself!

In 1976, Steve and a college friend, Steve Wozniak, founded Apple Computers®. Steve Wozniak was a technical genius who had invented and built his own computer.

Jobs (left) with Wozniak (right)

At that time, computers were big and expensive. Steve Wozniak's was cheaper and smaller. Steve Jobs saw the potential of this invention, and helped Steve Wozniak to develop and sell it.

> **Did you know?**
>
> Apple's first office was in Steve Jobs' dad's garage in California. Today it is a tourist attraction.

The two Steves are credited with making computers popular for the home. However, by 1985 things weren't going so well. The company IBM (who had invented Grace Hopper's Mark I) had also made computers small enough to go into the home. They were popular and Apple was losing money. Steve Jobs left the company.

In the time that he was away, Steve continued developing technology. He bought a computer graphics company that became Pixar© studios – the company behind films such as *Finding Nemo* and *Toy Story*.

Steve returned to Apple in 1997 and helped to turn it into the company it is today. Steve designed new and popular Apple devices including music players, tablets and phones. Apple became a leader in modern mobile technology – his designs were easy for people to pick up and use!

Did you know?

In 2017, over 500,000 Apple phones were sold every day!

Steve Jobs bought the company that became Pixar for £3.8 million.

21 years later, Pixar was sold to Disney for £5.6 billion.

Steve was a game changer because he helped to create technology that people really wanted. Nowadays, most grown-ups have a phone, tablet or computer with them wherever they go.

Before Steve, this didn't really happen. He changed the way people use computers and technology. It was no longer just for computer geeks – it was for everybody! Steve Jobs Day is celebrated every October 16th in California, to remember Steve and what he did for the world.

Tim Berners-Lee

(1955–)

"The web is more a social creation than a technical one. I designed it... to help people work together."

Tim Berners-Lee

If you have ever surfed the **World Wide Web**, then you have Tim Berners-Lee to thank. He is the British computer scientist who invented it. Nowadays you can do anything on the web – from booking holidays to playing games and researching your homework! It's hard to imagine a time when the world wasn't at the end of your fingertips.

Did you know?

About 4 billion people use the **Internet** today.

Tim didn't invent the Internet. The Internet already existed, however Tim's game-changing moment was to find a way to open up the Internet to everybody.

Born in London, England in 1955, Tim was always interested in science and technology. He studied physics at Oxford University, and in 1980 he started work for CERN.

CERN

CERN is the European Organisation for Nuclear Research — a place where the best physicists and engineers try to discover more about how the universe works.

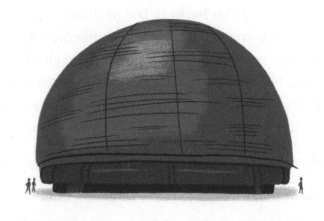

Tim loved railways as a boy. He learned about electronics through building model railways.

Tim wasn't at CERN to do research. Tim's job was to find new ways for CERN scientists to share the research they did with each other. It was at this time that he started using **hypertext**. Hypertext was one of the key features of the World Wide Web. It allowed users to share information quickly and easily.

When you click on a link in a website, you're using hypertext.

By 1989, Tim had figured out that if he could combine hypertext with the Internet, he could create a World Wide Web – web pages linked with each other through hypertext allowed users to 'surf the web'.

In 1991, the World Wide Web was officially born when the first website went live.

It wasn't as simple as just inventing the World Wide Web. Like Grace and Sarah before him, Tim had to find ways to make the web easy for everyone to use. Most importantly, Tim told everyone how to create their own web pages for free. He wanted the whole world to have access to the Internet so that anybody could build their own website and help the web to grow.

Game changers don't come much bigger than Tim. The World Wide Web has changed the way we do many things as a society. In 2004, Tim was **knighted** in honour of his achievements.

In 2012, Tim took part in the London Olympics opening ceremony. He tweeted a message to the world from the ceremony – 'This is for everyone.' – something that would have been impossible without his invention.

Nowadays, Tim spends his time teaching others and working to keep the Internet free for everyone.

Bill Gates

(1955–)

"The advance of technology is based on making it fit in so you don't really even notice it, so it's part of everyday life."

Bill Gates

Bill Gates is the university **drop-out** who **co-founded** the world's largest **software** company. Along the way, he became one of the richest people in the world. But that's just half of the story. Since 2008, he has devoted himself to charity and has promised to give away at least half of his fortune.

Did you know?

One of Bill's charity projects is a machine that can turn sewage into water that is safe for humans to drink.

Before we get into the details, here's a little statistic that will give you an idea of how rich Bill is. It is said that he earns $114 per second. That means, in the time it's taken you to read this sentence, he's made $300! That's about £230!

Gates (left) and Allen (right)

Bill earned his money by co-founding Microsoft with his friend Paul Allen in 1975. Microsoft is a software company. If you've ever used a computer, you've probably used a Microsoft product.

Computers don't work on their own – you need programs to be able to tell them what to do! Software is the name we give to programs that make computers work. Bill was brilliant at creating software.

He became interested in computers while at school. One of the first programs he wrote allowed you to play noughts and crosses against the computer.

> **Did you know?**
>
> Bill Gates loved board games as a child – his favourites were Risk™ and Monopoly™.

Bill met Paul Allen at school. At school, they made their first piece of software – a program that helped the school to timetable lessons.

When Bill and Paul founded Microsoft, Bill developed the software. He believed that one day, computers would be in lots of homes and businesses, and he knew that people would need software to make those computers work. Bill realised that if he could make the software for those computers, he would be a rich man! His plan worked.

Bill's game-changing moment came when he realised that he didn't have to make the computers themselves – he simply had to invent the software that made them work. By 1983, Microsoft software was on 30% of the world's computers. Today it is estimated to be on over 90%.

> **Did you know?**
>
> In 1998, Bill Gates appeared in an episode of the cartoon *The Simpsons*. He didn't provide the voice though – that was done by someone else.

In the past, software was on floppy disks like this.

In 2000, Bill and his wife set up the Bill and Melinda Gates Foundation. This is a charity that uses Bill and Melinda's money to help good causes. Since 2008, Bill has been working full time on the foundation. He has become known as much for his charity work as he has for his work with Microsoft.

Did you know?

Bill Gates still finds the time to read 50 books per year – I wonder if he'll read this one?

In 2010, Bill created and signed The Giving Pledge. This pledge means Bill has promised to donate at least half of his wealth to charity.

Bill Gates is a game changer who has changed the world with the invention of Microsoft Windows. He continues to change the world by donating a large amount of his wealth to the people who need it most.

Did you know?

It is estimated that Bill has donated £38 billion to charity over the last 25 years.

Larry Page and Sergey Brin

(1973–*)

"We want Google to be the third half of your brain."

<u>Sergey Brin</u>

"If you're changing the world ... then you're excited to get up in the morning."

<u>Larry Page</u>

The story of Sergey Brin and Larry Page is the story of Google™. Google is the world's most well-used Internet search engine. To 'Google' something has become so well-used that it is even in the Oxford English Dictionary!

* They were born in the same year, but they are not twins!

Sergey and Larry didn't invent the idea of an Internet search engine. Their game-changing moment happened when they came up with a new way to do the search.

Before Google, when you typed something into a search engine you got all the results that engine could find. Sergey and Larry came up with a way of ordering those results so that the most useful appeared at the top. When you used Google, you were more likely to find the information you needed quickly.

This game-changing idea began as a computer experiment when Larry and Sergey met at university in 1995. They worked in their university bedrooms, filling one room with computer equipment and using the other for programming. They invented their new search engine and made it available to their fellow students. In 1998, they made it available to the rest of the world – the rest is history!

Did you know?

Sergey and Larry have made so much money from Google that they have bought their own plane!

Even though they worked together to make Google, Larry and Sergey came from different places in the world. Larry was born and raised in the USA. Sergey was born in Russia and moved to the USA when he was six. Their invention has made them both billionaires, and they use their money to invest in new technology ideas.

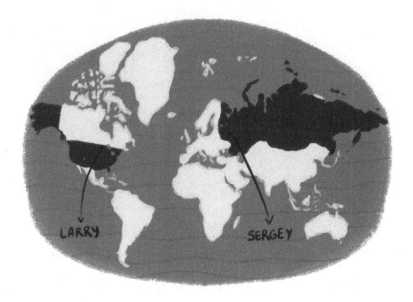

LARRY

SERGEY

Did you know?

Larry once made a printer out of Lego™!

Google has grown from two people working in a university bedroom to a massive industry. It now employs over 88,000 people, and its head office is so big that employees use brightly-coloured bicycles to get from one side to the other!

Google's head office in California

It is said 40,000 people use the Google search engine every second! Sergey and Larry changed the game with Google. They didn't just invent a search engine, they invented a whole new word!

Looking to the future

All of the computer wizards in this book wanted to take complicated ideas and make them easy to use. They have all helped to make technology become part of our lives in the 21st century. It just goes to show that sometimes the biggest ideas are about finding the simplest solutions.

What big problem do you think needs solving in the world today? Who knows – solve it and you might be in a book of the future!

 # Glossary

atomic bomb	a large bomb that uses nuclear technology
co-founded	to start something with another person
drop-out	someone who abandons their studying before finishing it
enlisted	joined the armed forces
formidable	very impressive and capable
hypertext	text that when clicked on takes you to another page on the Internet
icons	little pictures that you click on to give instructions to a computer
Internet	a network connecting millions of computers around the world
knighted	to be honoured by the Queen of the UK
mentored	to be advised or trained
pixel	the smallest area of colour that makes up a digital picture
revolutionised	changed something completely
software	programs used by a computer
World Wide Web	millions of interlinked/connected web pages

Index

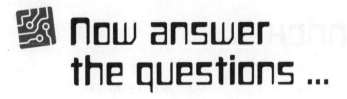

Now answer the questions ...

1 What surprising thing was named after Grace Hopper?

2 What does the word 'formidable' mean on page 3?

3 What unusual material did Larry Page once make a printer out of?

4 What do you think not having a television did for Shigeru?

5 Sum up the main way Susan Kare changed computing, using just one sentence.

6 Why do you think Tim Berners-Lee wanted to make the World Wide Web available for free to everyone?

7 Name two ways Bill Gates has changed the world. Which do you think is most important?

8 How many of the inventions and ideas in this book do you use every day?